Essays

JAPA

Swami Dayananda Saraswati
Arsha Vidya

Arsha Vidya
Research and Publication Trust
Chennai

Published by :

Arsha Vidya Research and Publication Trust
4 ' Sri nidhi' Apts 3rd Floor
Sir Desika Road, Mylapore
Chennai   600 004 INDIA
Tel   : 044 2499 7023
Telefax : 044 2499 7131
Email   : avrandpt@gmail.com
Website : www.avrpt.com

© Swami Dayananda Saraswati
   Arsha Vidya

All Rights Reserved.
No part of this book may be reproduced or transmitted in any form or by any means, electronic or mechanical, including photocopying, recording, or by any information storage and retrieval system, without written permission from the author and the publisher.

ISBN : 978–81–906059–9–1

First Edition	: May	2009	Copies : 5000
1st Reprint	: May	2012	Copies : 1000
2nd Reprint	: January	2013	Copies : 2000

Design & Layout :
Graaphic Design

Printed at :
Sudarsan Graphics
27, Neelakanta Mehta Street
T. Nagar
Chennai 600 017
Email : info@sudarsan.com

Contents

TALK 1

Meaning of *japa*	7
Unpredictability of thoughts	7
Pattern of thinking	8
Learning about the mind	10
Japa as a technique	11
Interval between thoughts	12
Peace in the mind	13
Restlessness requires a build-up	14
Beginning of thoughts	15
Occupation for the mind	16
Mind as a dancer	17
Nature of thought and silence	18
I am silence	19
Japa helps to nip a thought in its bud	19
Chant and the interval	21

TALK 2

Sound as a technique	23
Gāyatrī mantra	25
A meaningful chant	26

KEY TO TRANSLITERATION AND PRONUNCIATION OF SANSKRIT LETTERS

Sanskrit is a highly phonetic language and hence accuracy in articulation of the letters is important. For those unfamiliar with the *Devanāgarī* script, the international transliteration is a guide to the proper pronunciation of Sanskrit letters.

अ	a	(b*u*t)		ट	ṭa	(*t*rue)*3
आ	ā	(f*a*ther)		ठ	ṭha	(an*th*ill)*3
इ	i	(*i*t)		ड	ḍa	(*d*rum)*3
ई	ī	(b*ea*t)		ढ	ḍha	(go*dh*ead)*3
उ	u	(f*u*ll)		ण	ṇa	(u*n*der)*3
ऊ	ū	(p*oo*l)		त	ta	(pa*th*)*4
ऋ	ṛ	(*r*hythm)		थ	tha	(*th*under)*4
ॠ	ṝ	(ma*ri*ne)		द	da	(*th*at)*4
ऌ	ḷ	(reve*lr*y)		ध	dha	(brea*the*)*4
ए	e	(pl*ay*)		न	na	(*n*ut)*4
ऐ	ai	(*ai*sle)		प	pa	(*p*ut) 5
ओ	o	(g*o*)		फ	pha	(loo*ph*ole)*5
औ	au	(lo*u*d)		ब	ba	(*b*in) 5
क	ka	(see*k*) 1		भ	bha	(a*bh*or)*5
ख	kha	(bloc*kh*ead)*1		म	ma	(*m*uch) 5
ग	ga	(*g*et) 1		य	ya	(lo*y*al)
घ	gha	(lo*g h*ut)*1		र	ra	(*r*ed)
ङ	ṅa	(si*ng*) 1		ल	la	(*l*uck)
च	ca	(*ch*unk) 2		व	va	(*v*ase)
छ	cha	(cat*ch h*im)*2		श	śa	(*s*ure)
ज	ja	(*j*ump) 2		ष	ṣa	(*sh*un)
झ	jha	(he*dgeh*og)*2		स	sa	(*s*o)
ञ	ña	(bu*nch*) 2		ह	ha	(*h*um)

˙	ṁ	*anusvāra*	(nasalisation of preceding vowel)
:	ḥ	*visarga*	(aspiration of preceding vowel)
*			No exact English equivalents for these letters

1. Guttural – Pronounced from throat
2. Palatal – Pronounced from palate
3. Lingual – Pronounced from cerebrum
4. Dental – Pronounced from teeth
5. Labial – Pronounced from lips

The 5th letter of each of the above class – called nasals – are also pronounced nasally.

TALK 1

Meaning of japa

Japa is the repetition of a word or short sentence during meditation. The letter *ja* stands for that which puts an end to the cycle of birth and death and the letter *pa* stands for that which removes or destroys all impurities and obstructions. Therefore, *japa* is an indirect means for liberation, *mokṣa*. By destroying the varieties of obstructions to knowledge, *japa* paves the way for liberation.[1] *Japa*, then, is more than a mere discipline or technique.

These two talks will give one an understanding of the nature and logic of *japa* and the way it works. With this understanding one would be able to do *japa* with conviction and handle it properly.

Unpredictability of thoughts

At any given time, one has only one thought; what is the next thought is anyone's guess. But when the next thought does occur, it will have done so because of some logic. In chain thinking there is no thought without certain connection to the

---

[1] *jakāro janma-viccheddaḥ pakāraḥ pāpanāśanaḥ
Janmakarmaharo yasmāt tasmājjapa iti smṛtaḥ.*

preceding thought. This connection may be flimsy or it may be very clear and logical. But the thought itself is never predictable.

Even now, I cannot predict what I am going to say. I simply said I would talk on *japa*, and started. Even the words I am saying right now were not known to me. What is going to come is unpredictable, but when it does come, it has the backing of logic, reason.

Pattern of thinking

Suppose you see a BMW on the road and it draws your attention. What will your next thought be?

"How can he afford it?"

And then,

"How can he afford such an expensive car? Last year he did not even have a job. His wife must have a lot of money. I wish my wife came from a rich family. When I got married I did not think about money or my future." (Laughter).

All these thoughts started from seeing a BMW and they follow certain logic. This particular sequence is only one line of thinking.

Let us look at another one, the sight of BMW.

"The German people are quite industrious. Even though their country was devastated during World War II, their economy rebounded quickly. They produce the best scientific equipments in the world."

Where did you start? From BMW. What will come after BMW is anybody's guess. Even in deliberate thinking you do not know what is coming next because thinking is always linear, one step at a time, one thought at a time. The connection between thoughts can either be a logical, syntactical connection within a sentence or a simple association. But there will always be a connection, weak or strong.

In 'BMW thinking,' the connection between thoughts is not a deliberate one. Therefore, the next thought can be anything. "The BMW emblem is different. It is not like the Mercedes insignia." The Mercedes insignia makes you think of a star and then the next thought can be, "My astrological sign is not favourable." This movement from one thought to the next is listless thinking, a meandering of thoughts in which there is no direction.

In listless thinking, although there is no direction, there is always some logic, some connection. It may be a simple rhyme, one word reminding you of another, or a variety of other possible connections. The one invariable is that, at any given time, there is always one thought or another in your mind.

Just as in deliberate thinking, in listless thinking also, one does not know what one's next thought is. But, in *japa* one definitely knows what is coming next. The *japa* can be a word, a short sentence, a section of a Veda, but to be a *japa* it must be repeated.

If one is repeating a word or short sentence one is sure about when one is off track. In 'BMW thinking,' however, to think of Germany and then of a Mercedes or anything else is not to go off track because there is no track. Such thinking just happens. This is what listless thinking means. There is no direction to it.

Learning about the mind

We really do not have a method to learn about the mind. We only know that we are subjected to a particular type of thinking. For example, we get into a reverie until something arrests our attention and only then do we come back.

Is there anything that we have in our thought life, which is our life, which helps us understand our ways of thinking? What do we have to help us learn how to direct our thinking for a given length of time and have the mind at our disposal?

We have no directed technique. If we were lucky, we would have acquired some intellectual discipline in school which has given us the capacity for logical thinking. In the process, we may have discovered some discipline, but we do not know it is a technique; nor do we use it as one.

Japa as a technique

Exercising choice is very important in *japa*. If I choose to mentally chant a word or a sentence for a length of time, then I have a technique in hand and can see what happens in my mind because I know exactly what is to come next. If something else pops up, I know this is not what is expected and I bring back the chosen thought. In the process I learn how to dismiss unwanted thoughts and retain the one I have chosen. This is one important result of *japa* as a technique.

As a technique, any word will work. You do not require the Lord's name or a 'spiritual' *mantra*. Any sound can be a *mantra*, like 'gring... gring... gring.... gring... gring... gring....' If you keep on repeating this sound, it will work. An extraneous thought will eventually come, like, "What makes this kind of noise?" "A bagpipe," may be the response. Then you may ask, "What does a bagpipe have to do with my *japa*?" By returning to the sound, the bagpipe thought is dismissed.

Thus, repetition works as a technique for gaining some mental discipline; you give yourself an occasion to see the ways of your own thinking. But *japa* of a meaningful chant invokes the basic person in you. You have to be this person while doing *japa*.

Interval between thoughts

The advantage of repetition is that you can appreciate the interval between two successive occupations of the mind. In listless thinking with no direction, the mind simply moves from one thought to another. This type of thinking is like picking up noodles. If you try to pick up one noodle, you find it coming along with a few others. Similarly, the whole occupation of thinking becomes 'as though' a single thought, even though there are many thoughts.

Between two thoughts there is an interval. BMW is the name of a vehicle and Germany is the name of a country. Because there is a connection between the two, the interval between them is missed. Repeating a given chant eliminates or avoids the connection between two thoughts because, between one chant and another, there is no connection.

Each chant is a complete unit in itself and one thought unit is not connected to the second thought unit since both are the same. Thus, between two chants, there is a period; chant... Period... chant... Period. There is no comma, only period, a full stop. Therefore, each chant is complete and, between chants, the interval is available for you to recognise.

Peace in the mind

What is it that obtains in the interval between chants? Between one thought with certain form and sound and the next thought, there is no given thought. There is only an interval with no form or shape. This is what we call peace or silence. Because this silence has no particular thought form, there is no thinking as we know it.

We always think that peace is something we have to acquire. People even ask for it: "Swamiji, I have everything except peace of mind. How can I gain this peace?" Because the mind is restless, we think that peace is something new that we have to acquire, an attribute with which we have to embellish the mind. Is peace something we have to acquire or is it natural?

I once went to a swami. I could sense that he was a person who was at peace with himself. I had committed myself to Vedanta but, at the same time, I had a lot of conflicts in my pursuit. I went to this swami in an attempt to resolve them. He never talked much, but he said one thing to me that really hit home: "For restlessness, you have to work a lot. For peace, what is there to do?" Having asked this question, he became silent, which I found to be very effective.

Restlessness requires a build-up

For peace, what do you have to do? For restlessness you have to work; you have to create a build-up because, without one, you can never become restless. The problem is that this build-up is not something that we do consciously. It gets built up, like a wall erecting itself. Suppose you have a pile of bricks and they just assemble themselves into a wall. You would consider it a miracle, but you do not consider a build-up of thoughts a miracle because it is always happening. It is a miracle because it just happens. That it just builds itself up and you have no say over it; it is truly amazing!

There is helplessness in the whole process. Something triggers off a build-up; it may be a simple hormonal change, indigestion, someone's look, a frown, a change of weather, or any number of other things. Any one thing is good enough; you may be combing your hair and a few hairs come out! Any event that you do not accept starts it off and then your mind is busy for the entire day.

Restlessness requires a build-up to which I, myself, am not a party. Yet the build-up is mine. I do not look upon it as different from myself. I see myself fuming.

Why is it that I cannot keep track of this thought-by-thought build-up? This is because the whole habit of thinking has been 'noodle thinking,' associative or non-directional thinking.

Beginning of thoughts

If I were to give the popular advice, "do not allow this type of thinking to build-up, just nip it in its bud," it would be easier said than done because there is no bud. The thinking first appears as a flower. By the time I become aware of it, it has become a huge jungle. It is not something that buds and can be nipped immediately.

The very beginning of such thinking is an association of I. Without that, the thoughts would not begin. This mechanical thinking, associated as it is with I, has no history, really. We may say it comes from childhood, that we picked it up from our parents, which means that they picked it up from their parents, and so on. If that is the case, this kind of thinking has no actual beginning; it is not created at a given time.

Because of its association with 'I' there is no question of my being aware of the first thought because I am taken over at the outset by the thinking itself. I become the very thought and the thought becomes me.

Therefore, the advice, 'nip it in its bud,' is meaningless and can only create a complex; "I cannot nip it in its bud, so I am no good." Such thinking just adds to my build-up of guilt. What, then, can I do?

Occupation for the mind

I can give the mind a meaningful occupation wherein chain thinking is broken. Then the interval that obtains between successive thoughts can reveal a great fact about myself: I am the silence that obtains between two thoughts.

Logically, I can see how restlessness requires a build-up, whereas peace is something very natural for which I need not do anything. I do not create peace; I create only restlessness.

In *japa*, I deliberately create a thought. Because I have a will, I can choose. In this way, I become the author of a given thought. I create a specific thought because I choose it, whereas the silence ensues is not created by me. In fact, the silence is the basis of all thoughts.

Mind as a dancer

In the book, *Pañcadaśī*,[2] the mind is likened to a dancer on a lighted stage.

---

[2] Chapter 10 (*nāṭaka-dīpa-prakaraṇam*)

The dancer portrays a variety of aesthetic sentiments: love, helplessness, anger, cruelty, wonderment, and fright. The light on the stage lights up the dancer, her moods and the relevant changes; when she exits, it lights up the empty stage. The dancer may be performing various dance forms, or may not be on the stage at all, yet the light remains uninvolved. It merely illumines.

The light itself is not a doer, much less an enjoyer of the dance. Nor does it light up the stage as one of its jobs. The nature of light is to illumine and it illumines; the verb 'illumines' involves no action or motive on the part of the light. Therefore, the light has no doer-ship. Similarly, when I have a thought and the thought goes away, what remains is silence, which is likened to the empty stage without a dancer.

Nature of thought and silence

Absence of thought is generally looked upon as peace, something to be achieved. Thought can be suppressed or negated by certain external means, such as the practice of breath control. When you retain the breath, you cannot think. Try. Hold your nose and try to think. You cannot. Your only thought is to breathe!

Here, however, we are not interested in the absence of thought but in understanding the nature of thought and silence. The whole approach, therefore, is cognitive. Thought sometimes happens without my sanction and sometimes it happens with my sanction. In *japa*, thought is deliberate; it occurs with my sanction. And when the thought goes, I understand its absence as the nature of silence.

I am silence

What I experience, or am aware of, between two thoughts is silence. If I see the silence after every thought, should I take myself to be the thought or should I take myself to be the silence? Thought arises and thought falls. Before the rise of the thought I am silence and after the departure of the thought I am silence. I am silence first and I am silence last, meaning that in spite of thoughts, I am silence.

The practice of *japa* does not give me this understanding. But, by doing *japa*, I create a situation wherein something that is understood becomes clearer. In spite of thoughts, I understand, I am silence.

Japa helps to nip a thought in its bud

By doing *japa*, you learn how to nip a thought in its bud. Just as you see poison ivy,[3] you do not let it grow, so too, by being aware of the interval between thoughts, you gain the capacity to nip a thought in the bud.

In 'BMW thinking' you hold onto the next thought and leaves the previous; Then, again you hold on to the next, leaving the previous. The lingering content of the initial thought connects you to the next thought. This connection causes the process to move from BMW to Germany. Germany to World War II, World War II to Pearl Harbour and Pearl Harbour takes you to Hawaii. Hawaii takes you to the beach. The beach takes you to melanoma[4] and you become sad.

This is how the mind works. If you catch one thought, it means the previous one is gone because the two thoughts have

---

[3] Poison Ivy grows under the shade of a tree, whose leaves cause painful blisters in contact with one's skin. They are all over the east coast of U.S.A

[4] Skin cancer due to sun-bathing

nothing to do with each other, save some lingering connection. This is why, so often, you lose track of where you began in a conversation.

The reason you cannot keep track of where you began in a conversation is that you do not hold the wheel; conversation just takes place. You may start talking about the country's foreign policy and end up discussing sweepstakes. In between many other topics come up. There is no control and you do not know how it all happened. The flimsier the connections, the more difficult it is to relate one thought to another.

I call this type of thinking 'monkey thinking,' the mind being very much like a monkey who leaps from tree to tree. One tree may be an evergreen and the next a maple. The monkey just goes from one to the other. Similarly, one's mind jumps from thought to thought and there is no control over the ways of one's thinking. In this kind of chain thinking, one cannot arrive at the gap, the interval that exists between thoughts.

Chant and the interval

In India there is a tree called the areca tree, from which we get the betel nut. It is like a tall and thin coconut tree, tapering at the top and fibrous. Looking at the tree you may think it will break if you climb it, but it will not. A man who goes up this tree to gather bunches of fruits at the top does not need to come down and climb another tree. Instead, by bending the tree with his own bodyweight, he catches hold of the adjacent tree. In this way, he catches hold of the adjacent tree. And he moves from tree to tree-gathering fruits. Only after picking the fruits from the last tree in the garden does he come down!

This is exactly what we do in our thinking, going from one thought to the next. It is like walking upon thoughts; you never get to the ground.

Whereas, the coconut tree will never bend. A man picking coconuts must return to the ground before climbing the next tree. *Japa* is the same. You get to the ground, not after a length of time, but immediately. You chant and you come down. Chant... Come down. Chant.... Come down.... Chant.... Come down. In this type of chanting to be aware of the interval is as important as the chant because it is the interval that reveals your true nature which is silence, consciousness.

TALK 2

Once you are committed to repeating a given chant mentally, your mind automatically goes to *japa* whenever it is free. Just as water draining from the mountains creates new ravines, a new track of healthy habit is created towards which the mind goes, repeatedly. In this way, *japa* becomes a way of keeping the mind meaningfully, prayerfully occupied. Eventually, a time comes when the mind enjoys certain composure. You begin to appreciate that any distraction or agitation is but transitory and you do not come under its spell. In conjunction with the vision of the teaching that 'you are the whole,' *japa* is very effective. Even without any exposure to Vedanta, *japa* is beneficial in that it keeps the mind meaningfully occupied.

Sound as a technique

A common practice among those who practice meditation in the West is to chant invocatory syllables, called *bījākṣaras*—*śrīm, hrīm, aim* and so on, which are traditionally used to invoke particular deities. When these sounds or any other single syllable words, such as *Rām* and *Śyām* are chanted, the mind is naturally going to have a particular occupation. Because the chant is repetitive, chain thinking is eliminated.

One scientist demonstrated that any sound could work as a technique, by using a meaningless sound and recording changes in various human functions. While the subject chanted this sound, his thought processes and metabolism slowed down significantly. His blood pressure also came down and his heart beat rhythmically.

Since the person was sitting quietly, his mind occupied with the repetition of the meaningless sound, these findings are not surprising. Had he thought of some problem he had, he would have begun to fume and naturally his heartbeat would have increased. Based on the results of his study, the scientist wrote a paper in which he concluded that a special chant or *mantra* was not required and that the repetition of any sound, even a meaningless sound, could produce the benefits he had recorded.

As a technique, any sound that is repeated will work as well as any other sound. But in what way will it work? For sometime, no doubt, the body and the mind will be quieter. But then, you may become amused that you are sitting and chanting a meaningless sound. Is it not amusing to set aside a time each day to chant gring... gring.... gring so seriously?

I know I would be amused. Something would tell me, "idiot! What are you doing?" and I would reply, "Be quiet. You always criticise. You don't believe in anything. Keep chanting." I would resume, 'gring, gring, gring.'

Someone would ask from inside:

"What is this gring?"

"It's a meaningless sound,"

"A meaningless sound? Why are you chanting a meaningless sound?"

"It's called.... Be quiet. I told you not to criticise."

"Gring... gring... gring... gring."

"Did you pay for this? Why don't you change gring into zring or some other sound?"

"Be quiet! This sound was specially chosen for me. Gring... gring... gring."

It would be very difficult for me to chant this meaningless sound.

Anything you do should be meaningful. It is very difficult, therefore, to seriously sit and chant a meaningless sound. One may not know the proper meaning of a chant, but one needs to know that it is meaningful. If it is the Lord's name, one may not understand its full meaning, but because one knows it means the Lord, one has enough understanding to chant it seriously.

Gāyatrī mantra

In India, it is quite common for a child to be initiated into a *mantra*, called *Gāyatrī*. The person who initiated me into *Gāyatrī* did not teach me its entire meaning. He only said that it was a prayer asking the Lord to give us a bright mind. Although I was not given its entire meaning, it was given as a prayer to be done three times a day. Later, of course, I gained an appreciation of its meaning.

Therefore, this *mantra* and others serve as a technique, enabling a young child to learn how to use his or her mind. It works because, when the child chants the *mantra*, the mind will wander. The child then directs it back to the chant, thereby learning how to use the mind. At a young age a child gets an insight into his or her mind, which is not an ordinary thing. To know how the mind works is a great blessing.

A meaningful chant

If you chant a sound that has no meaning it can serve as a technique. And for the reasons I have mentioned, it looks as though any chant will work. But all sounds that you repeat will not work because you cannot give meaning to a chant that is meaningless and, therefore, you cannot be serious about it.

Suppose, however, you chant a word that does have a meaning like carrot: carrot... carrot... carrot.... carrot. Even though it is meaningful, carrot does not have the power to invoke the basic person who is free from being an enjoyer and a doer. Instead, you choose one meaningful word that covers the whole creation, a word that is not one of the many objects in the world. A meaningless sound does not indicate any object, whereas a meaningful sound revealing the Lord's name includes everything without indicating any one object. Since all objects are included in the form of the Lord, nothing is omitted when you repeat the Lord's name.

Thus, the meaningful chant becomes all-inclusive. All words are included in one chosen word. All names in all languages are also included. Traditionally, the word can vary, but in your understanding the word chosen should stand for everything. Since the word does not stand for a particular thing, you will not be reminded of a given object when you chant it.

Morevoer, you are related to the Lord whose name you repeat. As the basic person you are related to the whole, the Lord. You are a devotee and the altar of your devotion is recognised in a form or a name. Since you live up in a given religious culture, you recognise certain names as those of the Lord. The bridge in your psyche is a blessing because these names immediately strike your mind as the Lord. Further, through education, a given name can become connected in your mind to signify the Lord.

In relation to the meaning of a word known to you as the Lord, you are a devotee. The devotee is the fundamental person who assumes a variety of relative roles such as father/mother, wife/husband, brother/sister and so on. If you are an individual, you are first related to the total and, only later are you related to different individuals within the total. And the total is the Lord.

The total being the basis for the individual, my relationship with the Lord is fundamental. This basic relationship makes me a devotee. Related to any given person I become a devotee-son or a devotee daughter. The devotee assumes a role.

When I chant the name of the Lord, I play no role; I am the basic person; I am a devotee. In the devotee-Lord relationship there will be none of the distractions attached to the relative roles assumed by the devotee.

There are words that sometimes are chanted, that are not *mantra*s at all; *Śivo' ham* ... *Śivo' ham* or *So'ham*, meaning, 'He I am,' 'He' referring to the Lord. Nowhere in the scriptures does it say that *so'ham* is a *mantra*. *So'ham* is a fact. It is a sentence to be understood. It means 'I am He, the Lord.' If you are the Lord or if the Lord is you, there must be non-difference between the two. Because the differences are obvious to you, you need not inquire into them further. The non-difference is what you need to know and that is the subject matter of the entire teaching of Vedanta. Therefore, sentences that are statements of fact are not *mantra*s.

A *japa* is a word, sentence, or group of sentences, whose meaning is the Lord, wherein the individual invokes or salutes a particular deity as the Lord. It is neither a meaningless sound nor does it denote a particular object, like zucchini. Its meaning is the Lord, through which the devotee is invoked. Therefore, *japa* not only serves as a technique but also as a mental prayer. Only when the repetition is a mental prayer it is called *japa*.

Japa is recognised as an indirect means for gaining liberation because it destroys all obstructions and impurities, thereby preparing the mind for the knowledge that is liberation. In the tenth chapter of the *Bhagavad Gītā*, Lord Kṛṣṇa says, there are many forms of rituals and many means through which I am invoked, "But among the rituals I am *japa*."[5]

Japa, therefore, is something to be done and as the Lord himself, in the form of Kṛṣṇa, has said, there is no activity more efficacious than *japa*.

Oṁ tat sat

---

[5] *yajñānāṁ japayajño'smi* (*Bhagavad Gītā* 10.25)

BOOKS BY SWAMI DAYANANDA SARASWATI

Public Talk Series :

1. Living Intelligently
2. Successful Living
3. Need for Cognitive Change
4. Discovering Love
5. Value of Values
6. Vedic View and Way of Life

Upaniṣad Series :

7. Muṇḍakopaniṣad
8. Kenopaniṣad

Prakaraṇa Series :

9. Tattvabodhaḥ

Text Translation Series :

10. Śrīmad Bhagavad Gītā
    (Text with roman transliteration and English translation)

11. Śrī Rudram
    (Text in Sanskrit with transliteration, word-to-word and verse meaning along with an elaborate commentary in English)

Stotra Series :

12. Dīpārādhanā
13. Prayer Guide
    (With explanations of several Mantras, Stotras, Kirtans and Religious Festivals)

Moments with Oneself Series :

14. Freedom from Helplessness
15. Living versus Getting On
16. Insights
17. Action and Reaction
18. Fundamental Problem
19. Problem is You, Solution is You
20. Purpose of Prayer
21. Vedanta 24x7
22. Freedom
23. Crisis Management
24. Surrender and Freedom
25. Need for Personal Reorganisation
26. Freedom in Relationship
27. Stress-free Living
28. Om Namo Bhagavate Vāsudevāya
29. Yoga of Objectivity
30. Īśvara in One's Life

Bhagavad Gītā Series :

31. Bhagavad Gītā Home Study Course (Hardbound - 9 Volumes)

Meditation Series :

32. Morning Meditation Prayers
33. What is Meditation?

Essays :

34. Do all Religions have the same goal?
35. Conversion is Violence
36. Gurupūrṇimā
37. Dānam
38. Japa
39. Can We?
40. Moments with Krishna
41. Teaching Tradition of Advaita Vedanta
42. Compositions of Swami Dayananda Saraswati

Exploring Vedanta Series : (*vākya-vicāra*)

43. śraddhā bhakti dhyāna yogād avaihi ātmānaṁ ced vijānīyāt

Books translated in other languages and in English based on Swami Dayananda Saraswati's Original Exposition

Tamil

44. Veeduthorum Gitopadesam (9 Volumes)
    (Bhagavad Gītā Home Study Course)
45. Dānam

Kannada

46. Mane maneyalli Adhyayana
    (7 Volumes)
    (Bhagavad Gītā Home Study Course)

47. Vedanta Pravesike

Telugu

49. Kenopaniṣad

Hindi

50. Ghar baithe Gītā Vivechan (Vol 1)
    (Bhagavad Gītā Home Study Course)

51. Antardṛṣṭi (Insights)

52. Vedanta 24X7

53. Kriya aur Pratikriya
    (Action and Reaction)

Marathi

54. Gruhe Gītā Adhyayan
    (Vol 1 available)
    (Bhagavad Gītā Home Study Course)

English

55. The Jungian Myth and Advaita Vedanta

56. The Vedantic Self and the Jungian Psyche

57. Salutations to Rudra

58. Without a Second

Biography (Hardbound Deluxe)

> 59. Swami Dayananda Saraswati
>   Contributions & Writings
>   (Smt. Sheela Balaji)

Biography (Hardbound Regular)

> 60. Swami Dayananda Saraswati
>   Contributions & Writings
>   (Smt. Sheela Balaji)

Also available at :

ARSHA VIDYA RESEARCH
AND PUBLICATION TRUST
32 / 4 Sir Desika Road
Mylapore Chennai 600 004
Telefax : 044 - 2499 7131
Email : avrandpc@gmail.com
Website : www.avrpt.com

ARSHA VIDYA GURUKULAM
Anaikatti P.O.
Coimbatore 641 108
Ph : 0422 - 2657001
Fax : 0422 - 2657002
Email : office@arshavidya.in
Website : www.arshavidya.in

ARSHA VIDYA GURUKULAM
P.O.Box 1059. Pennsylvania
PA 18353, USA
Ph : 001 - 570 - 992 - 2339
Email : avp@epix.net
Website : www.arshavidya.org

SWAMI DAYANANDA ASHRAM
Purani Jhadi, P.B.No. 30
Rishikesh, Uttaranchal 249 201
Telefax : 0135 - 2430769
Email : ashrambookstore@yahoo.com
Website : www.dayananda.org

Other leading Book Stores:

Chennai:	**044**
Motilal Banarsidass	2498 2315
Giri Trading	2495 1966
Higginbothams	2851 3519
Pustak Bharati	2461 1345
Theosophical Publishing House	2446 6613 / 2491 1338
The Odessey	43910300

New Delhi: **011**
  Motilal Banarsidass   2385 8335/2385 1985/2385 2747

Bengaluru: **080**
- Gangarams — 2558 1617 / 2558 1618
- Sapna Book House — 4011 4455 / 4045 5999
- Strand Bookstall — 2558 2222, 2558 0000
- Vedanta Book House — 2650 7590

Coimbatore: **0422**
- Guru Smruti — 9486773793
- Giri Trading — 2541523

Trivandrum: **0471**
- Prabhus Bookhouse — 2478397 / 2473496

Kozhikode: **0495**
- Ganga Bookhouse — 6521262

Mumbai: **022**
- Chetana Bookhouse — 2285 1243 / 2285 3412
- Strand Bookstall — 2266 1994 / 2266 1719 / 2261 4613
- Giri Trading — 2414 3140

Bardoli (Surat): **0622**
- Dr. Anil Patwardhan — 220283
- (BGHS course - Marathi) 0-9377715684

Mysore :
- Swamini Varadananda — 0-9242890144
- (BGHS course - Kannada) 0-8762464014